Printed in Great Britain
by Amazon

61530090R00058